30 DAYS OF WORSHIP

BETTER IS ONE DAY DEVOTIONAL

Devotions Inspired by the Song

Inspiration and Motivation for the Seasons of Life

COOK COMMUNICATIONS MINISTRIES
Colorado Springs, Colorado • Paris, Ontario
KINGSWAY COMMUNICATIONS LTD
Eastbourne, England

Honor® is an imprint of
Cook Communications Ministries, Colorado Springs, CO 80918
Cook Communications, Paris, Ontario
Kingsway Communications, Eastbourne, England

BETTER IS ONE DAY
© 2006 by Honor Books

All rights reserved. No part of this book may be reproduced without written permission, except for brief quotations in books and critical reviews. For information, write Cook Communications Ministries, 4050 Lee Vance View, Colorado Springs, CO 80918.

Manuscript written by Adam Palmer
Cover Design BMB Design
Cover Photo © #899736 Index Stock Imagery, Inc.
Interior photo © Digital Vision

First Printing, 2006
Printed in Canada

1 2 3 4 5 6 7 8 9 10 Printing/Year 10 09 08 07 06

All Scripture quotations, unless otherwise noted, are taken from the *Holy Bible, New International Version*®. *NIV*®. Copyright © 1973, 1978, 1984 by International Bible Society. Used by permission of Zondervan. All rights reserved.

ISBN-13: 978-1-56292-815-5
ISBN-10: 1-56292-815-5

LCCN: 2005937825

Introduction

Everything in our society today is about what is better. Better this and better that. Upgraded. New and improved. Extra strength. Ultimate.

The best.

Our society is obviously sorely lacking in perspective. The Bible plainly tells us in poetic terms that a thousand days of improved teeth whitening and upgraded technology is still a mere paper airplane compared to just one day with the magnificent, soaring bird of God's greatness.

Matt Redman, author of a number of wonderful worship songs, has pulled some of these themes out of the book of Psalms and given us an insightful meditation on God and his simple "better-ness."

God is so much better than anything this world has to offer. Just one day with him outshines a thousand days with the best of the world. As you study his Word through this devotional, may you come to know how much better God is. May you experience a breakthrough in your perspective of God. May you long for just one day in his presence.

Better Is One Day

By Matt Redman

How lovely is Your dwelling place
O Lord Almighty
My soul longs and even faints for You
For here my heart is satisfied
Within Your presence
I sing beneath the shadow of Your wings

Better is one day in Your courts
Better is one day in Your house
Better is one day in Your courts
Than thousands elsewhere

One thing I ask and I would seek
To see Your beauty
To find You in the place Your glory dwells

My heart and flesh cry out
For You, the living God
Your Spirit's water for my soul
I've tasted and I've seen
Come once again to me
I will draw near to You
I will draw near to You

© 1995 Thankyou Music (PRS), administered worldwide by EMI CMG
Publishing, excluding Europe, which is administered by
kingswaysongs.com.

DAY 1: How Lovely Is Your Dwelling Place

The LORD said to Moses, "Tell the Israelites to bring me an offering. You are to receive the offering for me from each man whose heart prompts him to give. These are the offerings you are to receive from them: gold, silver and bronze; blue, purple and scarlet yarn and fine linen; goat hair; ram skins dyed red and hides of sea cows; acacia wood; olive oil for the light; spices for the anointing oil and for the fragrant incense; and onyx stones and other gems to be mounted on the ephod and breastpiece. Then have them make a sanctuary for me, and I will dwell among them."

—Exodus 25:1–8

Better is God's invitation.

Believe it or not, God wants to dwell with us.

God wants to step down from his dwelling place, from heaven, and spend time with his people. Quality time. We see it in the beginning when God sought out Adam in the garden of Eden (see Gen. 3:8–9). We know that in the end, God will bring all of us to spend eternity with him.

But God also wants to spend time with us now. He said to Moses that he will dwell with the Israelites. However, notice something earlier in this passage: "Receive the offering for me from each man whose heart prompts him to give." There is a requirement to receive God into one's presence.

We have to want it. And then we have to give up part of ourselves.

God is saying to the Israelites—and us—"I want you to be involved in this. I won't take over by force. I'm not going to elbow you out of the way and take up residence at your address. You have to show me you want me here. I want you to be part of this."

God's invitation to us is an invitation to give up something in return for his presence.

As an act of worship, he wants us to receive our gifts and return our worship in a way we could never imagine.

It starts with us.

Prayer for the Day:

Lord, thank you for your invitation. Thank you for giving me the direction I need, so that I know to invite you into my life. And thank you for fulfilling your end of the bargain. I prepare a place in my heart for you right now, Lord, and, as I worship you this day, I pray you will fill that place with your presence.

AMEN.

DAY 2: How Lovely Is Your Dwelling Place

You, however, are controlled not by the sinful nature but by the Spirit, if the Spirit of God lives in you. And if anyone does not have the Spirit of Christ, he does not belong to Christ. But if Christ is in you, your body is dead because of sin, yet your spirit is alive because of righteousness. And if the Spirit of him who raised Jesus from the dead is living in you, he who raised Christ from the dead will also give life to your mortal bodies through his Spirit, who lives in you.

—Romans 8:9–11

Better is God's nature.

Yesterday, we read about the Israelites and all the sacrifices they had to make in order to build a dwelling place for God. Flip back a few pages and check out all the things they had to bring as construction materials for the tabernacle. It's quite a list.

The ancient Israelites had to construct a dwelling place for God. They had to interact with him in a very limited way. They had rigid laws that were nearly impossible to keep.

We have none of those things.

Instead, *we* are his dwelling place.

Christ is in us. Instead of dwelling in a constructed facility, God now lives in us, giving us a righteousness the ancient Israelites could never attain. We have a life that we can never know outside of him.

And when we can approach him in honest worship, giving of ourselves, recognizing and honoring the Spirit of Christ that dwells within him, we become lovely. We become a temple more beautiful than anything anyone could build, no matter how precious the materials they used.

Prayer for the Day:

Lord Jesus, thank you for dwelling in me. If I really think about it, it kind of blows my mind, to be honest. But I know you live within me, so I pray that you'll help me to keep your temple clean. Help me to make your home a place where you feel welcome. In your precious name, Jesus.

AMEN.

DAY 3: O Lord Almighty

David said to the Philistine, "You come against me with sword and spear and javelin, but I come against you in the name of the LORD Almighty, the God of the armies of Israel, whom you have defied. This day the LORD will hand you over to me, and I'll strike you down and cut off your head. Today I will give the carcasses of the Philistine army to the birds of the air and the beasts of the earth, and the whole world will know that there is a God in Israel. All those gathered here will know that it is not by sword or spear that the LORD saves; for the battle is the LORD's, and he will give all of you into our hands." As the Philistine moved closer to attack him, David ran quickly toward the battle line to meet him. Reaching into his bag and taking out a stone, he slung it and struck the Philistine on the forehead. The stone sank into his forehead, and he fell facedown on the ground.

—1 SAMUEL 17:45–49

Better is God's protection.

First, a little bit of context: David was a shepherd boy, not a traditional soldier. Nevertheless, he trusted God for protection in his duties of sheep watching, once killing a bear and another time killing a lion—both times in order to keep his father's sheep safe.

So David had a history of defying the odds and seeing God protect him. He knew God's protection firsthand. He had seen the Lord Almighty go to work on his behalf.

Goliath the Philistine was doing something far worse than trying to steal sheep; he was insulting the very Lord Almighty who was responsible for protecting David. David heard Goliath's insults and went into shepherd mode.

He was going to take care of the trouble. He knew God would protect him.

What battles do we shy away from? How many times do we forget that God has proved himself over and over again to us? How often do we need to be reminded that God is a God of mercy and grace, yes, but he's also a God of might?

We know God will protect us, just like he protected David.

Addiction. Lust. Gossip. Anger. Bitterness. Resentment. Greed. These battles are not our own; they are the Lord's.

May we let go and let him fight for us. May we worship him for his protection.

Prayer for the Day:

Lord Almighty, thank you for your protective nature. Help me to trust in your might and not my own. Help me to step out and face my enemies. Remind me that my battles in life are not my own; they're yours. Through your strength and with your protection, I will win.

Amen.

DAY 4: My Soul Longs

O God, you are my God, earnestly I seek you; my soul thirsts for you, my body longs for you, in a dry and weary land where there is no water. I have seen you in the sanctuary and beheld your power and your glory. Because your love is better than life, my lips will glorify you. I will praise you as long as I live, and in your name I will lift up my hands.

—**PSALM 63:1–4**

Better is God's love.

What's the thirstiest you've ever been? Have you ever had one of those times where you had an enormous thirst but just couldn't find any way to quench it? There was no water around anywhere, nothing to drink at all. You just had to deal with your thirst and hope you could find some water somewhere.

Remember how wonderful it felt when you were finally able to slake your thirst?

Are you thirsty right now?

This is the feeling the psalmist is trying to portray. This is how our souls feel about God, though we can't always recognize it. And the way we satiate our soul's thirst is not through water, but through God's love.

When we come to him in worship, it's as if we are taking our thirsty souls to the wellspring of God's love and taking deep, long drinks.

> **God's love is better than life itself, and he's more than capable—and willing—to pour it out on us when we simply turn to him in worship and offer our meager cups. It is then that we can begin to understand what true soul satisfaction feels like.**

Prayer for the Day:

God, thank you so much for your love. Thank you for pouring it out so generously into my soul. Thank you for giving my soul what it so desperately needs to be satisfied. I worship you, Lord, and I offer my soul to you. Please fill it with your love. I need your love, Lord. I need it to feel complete. Thank you for giving it to me. I praise you.

Amen.

DAY 5: And Even Faints for You

When you go to war against your enemies and see horses and chariots and an army greater than yours, do not be afraid of them, because the LORD your God, who brought you up out of Egypt, will be with you. When you are about to go into battle, the priest shall come forward and address the army. He shall say: "Hear, O Israel, today you are going into battle against your enemies. Do not be fainthearted or afraid; do not be terrified or give way to panic before them. For the LORD your God is the one who goes with you to fight for you against your enemies to give you victory."

—**DEUTERONOMY 20:1–4**

Better is God's strength.

There's a part in the movie *A Bug's Life*, toward the end, when the evil grasshoppers are attacking our plucky ant heroes. Earlier in the film Dot, the youngest princess ant, encountered Thumper, the meanest grasshopper in the whole crew, and is already afraid of him.

So picture this scene. Dot and Thumper have this history together, where she's scared of him. And in the midst of the chaos of battle, the two run into each other. Thumper begins to make aggressive fighting noises at the small, defenseless ant, but she's unfazed. She even begins to threaten Thumper right back. Why? Because at that very moment, her friend Dim, an enormous rhino beetle, appears behind her and emits a powerful roar that frightens away Thumper and keeps Dot safe.

What a marvelous picture of God's strength.

Dot had no reason to be afraid of Thumper, because she knew Dim was backing her up.

Thumper didn't run from the fight because of Dot's threatening gestures; it was because of Dim's enormous strength, which obviously outmatched his.

In today's passage, we are encouraged not to grow faint when facing opposition that *appears* stronger. God told the priests to give the Israelite soldiers a little pep talk before the battle and remind them of what was really going on.

If there's anyone to grow faint toward, it's God.

**He is strong enough to fight for us.
He is the one we should worship.
He is the one we can trust.**

**He is the one for whom
we should grow faint.**

Prayer for the Day:

Dear God, help me know that you are always with me. Help my heart not to grow faint as I walk through life awaiting your return. Help me to let go and let you fight my battles, just as you fought for the Israelites. Lord, I'm sorry for growing faint at the wrong things; I choose to be impressed by you and only you. I love you, Lord.

AMEN.

DAY 6: For Here My Heart Is Satisfied

But I am the LORD your God, who brought you out of Egypt. You shall acknowledge no God but me, no Savior except me. I cared for you in the desert, in the land of burning heat. When I fed them, they were satisfied; when they were satisfied, they became proud; then they forgot me.

—HOSEA 13:4–6

Better is God's care.

It's so easy to get comfortable, isn't it?

Not necessarily at home, but in our spiritual lives. In our individual walks with God. It's so easy to get comfortable when our spiritual stomachs get full. It's so easy to forget that we need nourishment constantly.

God uses the picture of nourishment in this passage from the book of Hosea. Think about it. You can be ravenously hungry, but once you've satisfied that hunger with a delicious meal, the last thing you want to think about is the *next* meal. You're too wrapped up in enjoying the one you just had.

The same thing happened to the Israelites. There they were, wandering in the desert, when God reached down and cared for them. But once they were back to a comfortable state, they forgot how they got there.

How often do we do that? How often do we relax in our spirituality, especially when things are going well? Sure, we get into trouble, and then we call on God. But when everything's hunky-dory, how often do we forget about him?

What deserts has God brought you through? What's your story? How can you praise him for it?

His care for us is so much better than anything else we could possibly hope for. Let us not be like the Israelites described in Hosea; instead, let us offer our worship to him in remembrance of his caring hand.

Prayer for the Day:

God, please help me never forget the glorious day I gave my life to you. Help me share that day with others. Thank you for bringing me through my desert, Lord. I don't want to stay satisfied; I want to grow in you. I want more of you, Jesus.

AMEN.

DAY 7: For Here My Heart Is Satisfied

Jesus left there and went along the Sea of Galilee. Then he went up on a mountainside and sat down. Great crowds came to him, bringing the lame, the blind, the crippled, the mute and many others, and laid them at his feet; and he healed them. The people were amazed when they saw the mute speaking, the crippled made well, the lame walking and the blind seeing. And they praised the God of Israel. Jesus called his disciples to him and said, "I have compassion for these people; they have already been with me three days and have nothing to eat. I do not want to send them away hungry, or they may collapse on the way." His disciples answered, "Where could we get enough bread in this remote place to feed such a crowd?" "How many loaves do you have?" Jesus asked. "Seven," they replied, "and a few small fish." He told the crowd to sit down on the ground. Then he took the seven loaves and the fish, and when he had given thanks, he broke them and gave them to the disciples, and they in turn to the people. They all ate and were satisfied. Afterward the disciples picked up seven basketfuls of broken pieces that were left over. The number of those who ate was four thousand, besides women and children.

—**MATTHEW 15:29–38**

Better is God's satisfactory provision.

Here we have *more* hunger talk from God, but this time we see a miraculous example of Jesus wanting to meet our physical needs. It's a famous passage, this feeding of the crowds, and it happens more than once in the gospel of Matthew. One chapter before this one, there's the famous feeding of the five thousand with five loaves and two fish, and then there's this time where four thousand were fed with seven loaves and an undetermined number of fish.

But notice that in this passage (and in the previous chapter's miracle-food account), though the main miracle referenced was a supernatural multiplication of the food, other miracles were going on before that, mentioned in four brief words: "And he healed them."

Talk about a satisfied heart. Not only did the lame, the blind, the crippled, the mute, and many other people with physical afflictions get healed, but they also got a free dinner in the process!

God is all about our satisfaction, both in the physical sense and in the spiritual sense. There is no spiritual hunger he cannot satisfy, no spiritual healing he cannot perform. When we look to him in worship, offering our hungry spiritual bellies to him, he will provide us with spiritual nutrition, spiritual nourishment. He will satisfy our hearts.

All told, we know of at least nine thousand people in two chapters who found themselves satisfied by Christ's provision. Like them, we can find satisfaction only in him.

Prayer for the Day:

Lord Jesus, thank you for choosing to meet my needs. Thank you for providing satisfaction to my heart. Thank you. I'm so grateful for it. Help me not to stay satisfied, though. Help me to offer my heart to you again and again and again for renewal. I praise you for my satisfied heart. I love you.

AMEN.

DAY 8: Within Your Presence

Moses said to the LORD, "You have been telling me, 'Lead these people,' but you have not let me know whom you will send with me. You have said, 'I know you by name and you have found favor with me.' If you are pleased with me, teach me your ways so I may know you and continue to find favor with you. Remember that this nation is your people." The LORD replied, "My Presence will go with you, and I will give you rest." Then Moses said to him, "If your Presence does not go with us, do not send us up from here. How will anyone know that you are pleased with me and with your people unless you go with us? What else will distinguish me and your people from all the other people on the face of the earth?" And the LORD said to Moses, "I will do the very thing you have asked, because I am pleased with you and I know you by name." Then Moses said, "Now show me your glory." And the Lord said, "I will cause all my goodness to pass in front of you, and I will proclaim my name, the Lord, in your presence. I will have mercy on whom I will have mercy, and I will have compassion on whom I will have compassion. But," he said, "you cannot see my face, for no one may see me and live."

—Exodus 33:12–20

Better is God's favor.

It's game two of the American League Championship Series between the Chicago White Sox and the Los Angeles Angels. It's the bottom of the ninth inning, two outs, the score is tied, and White Sox player A. J. Pierzynski is at the plate, down two strikes. The ball is thrown, descends toward the dirt, and is caught as Pierzynski swings and misses. It's a strikeout.

Except that Pierzynski takes off toward first base and gets there, safe. Doug Eddings, the home-plate umpire, rules that Angels catcher Josh Paul didn't catch the pitch before it bounced and therefore Pierzynski needed to be touched with the ball for the Angels to get the out. Instead of a strikeout to end the inning, the White Sox now have a man on base.

Angels manager Mike Scioscia approaches Eddings to argue the call. However, the call stands, and the White Sox go on to win the game. There are just some arguments you'll never win.

Except with God. Moses begins to argue with God about the job he was given. Basically, Moses is saying to God, "This isn't fair! You're telling me to lead these people, but you're not helping me out here!"

And here's the interesting thing: It didn't hurt God's feelings. In fact, it established God's favor with Moses.

It's okay to ask for God's presence. It's okay to argue the call. God can take it, and while he may not overturn it, he will still love us. He will still envelop us in his presence, as long as we choose to ask him.

Let us praise him.

Prayer for the Day:

God, thanks for being so open with me. Thank you for listening to me when I vent my feelings in your direction. Thank you for accepting me for who I am, flaws and all. You see it all, Lord. You know my shortcomings. Help me to trust in your direction, and please extend your loving favor to me when I respectfully argue your call.

AMEN.

DAY 9: I Sing beneath the Shadow of Your Wings

Have mercy on me, O God, have mercy on me, for in you my soul takes refuge. I will take refuge in the shadow of your wings until the disaster has passed. I cry out to God Most High, to God, who fulfills his purpose for me. He sends from heaven and saves me, rebuking those who hotly pursue me; God sends his love and his faithfulness.

—Psalm 57:1–3

Better is God's refuge.

Shadows are not, in and of themselves, something to take refuge in. They are, after all, the absence of light. They are the by-product of a blockage of the sun or some other light source. It would be ridiculous to think that a shadow is something to seek when we are looking for refuge.

Shadows are indicators of refuge: The thing that is casting the shadow is the real refuge. And if we are underneath a shadow, then we are very close to the shadow's object. This psalm was written by David while he was on the run for his life from Saul, the king of Israel who wanted him dead. David was sitting in a cave when he wrote it, so he must have been keenly aware of shadows in that dimly lit place.

In the middle of his flight, David took a break and started singing of the shadow of God's wings. David understood that in taking refuge under a shadow, he was being covered by something mightier and bigger than himself.

It was a good time to worship.

In the midst of his refuge, David began to worship God, and in a matter of verses goes from "Have mercy on me, O God" to "God sends his love and his faithfulness." When we begin to worship God in our distress, he can focus us in the right direction quickly. David's circumstances didn't change—Saul was still out there looking for him—but God changed his inward focus and strengthened his spirit.

David was in the safest place he could be.

God's refuge is the safest place we can be. Let us sing under the shadow of his wings.

Prayer for the Day:

God, thank you for your refuge. Thank you for providing a safe place for me. Thank you for changing my heart, even when my outward circumstances don't change. I pray that you'll remind me, in the midst of my confusion, to stop and settle under your wings, to take a break and sing your praise. Thank you for your refuge and your peace.

AMEN.

DAY 10: Better Is One Day in Your Courts

When they heard this, they were furious and gnashed their teeth at him. But Stephen, full of the Holy Spirit, looked up to heaven and saw the glory of God, and Jesus standing at the right hand of God. "Look," he said, "I see heaven open and the Son of Man standing at the right hand of God." At this they covered their ears and, yelling at the top of their voices, they all rushed at him, dragged him out of the city and began to stone him. Meanwhile, the witnesses laid their clothes at the feet of a young man named Saul. While they were stoning him, Stephen prayed, "Lord Jesus, receive my spirit."

Then he fell on his knees and cried out, "Lord, do not hold this sin against them." When he had said this, he fell asleep.

—Acts 7:54–60

Better is God's message.

Stephen was a true early church warrior whose life was snuffed out way too early. Why? Because he had the nerve to share the love of Christ with an audience that just didn't want to hear it.

Stephen had, like Jesus before him, been falsely accused of speaking against the teachings of the Israelites, and in the fifty-three verses that precede today's passage, Stephen deftly defends himself and the gospel, placing it all in the context of the Judaism that the audience observed.

His words were spot-on, and they caused the crowd to become enraged. Instead of examining their own hearts, they took their anger out on Stephen and killed him then and there. Stephen gave up his life for the gospel, unwilling to settle for the slightest untruth about it.

How could he do such a thing? How could he give such an inflammatory speech that he knew would get him killed? Surely as he spoke his words, he could see the crowd stirring, beginning to be infuriated. Surely he knew he was placing himself in danger. Surely he knew that this would end badly. So why did he do it?

Because Stephen knew that just one truthful day in the courts of the Lord is better than a lifetime of compromise here. It wasn't a matter of trading his life for a single day in God's presence—that isn't really an option—but it was a matter of priorities. Stephen wanted to please God, because God had the strongest message.

Stephen wanted to stay true to the gospel, no matter what. He wanted to be loyal to God in the midst of his trials. He knew that God's message was the only one to die for.

God's courts are worth dying for, no matter what. May we do our best to die to ourselves and stay true to God's message.

Prayer for the Day:

God, I don't expect to die for you, really. I mean, I will, but I understand that your message is relatively accepted where I live. But I do know that it's hard to die to myself, to put my own ambitions and reputation on the line when it counts. Help me, Lord. Help me to stay loyal to your message, no matter what it might mean for me personally. No matter what it might do to my relationships. Remind me that your courts are better than anything I could ask for here.

AMEN.

DAY 11: Better Is One Day in Your House

[David] did not take the ark to be with him in the City of David. Instead, he took it aside to the house of Obed-Edom the Gittite. The ark of God remained with the family of Obed-Edom in his house for three months, and the LORD blessed his household and everything he had.

—1 CHRONICLES 13:13–14

Better is God's blessing.

So, here's the deal. The Philistines, enemies of Israel, had defeated the Israelite army and stolen the ark of God, the house where God resided. They carried it to their temple, and the next day, the idol of their god Dagon had fallen facedown in front of the ark. They replaced the idol, but the next day the same thing happened. Then they began to house the ark in other cities of Philistia, but everywhere they sent it, the people of that city would get horrible tumors.

The Philistines eventually got the idea and sent the ark back to Israel, where, after a series of events, it finally wound up at the home of Obed-Edom. This time, things were different. Instead of being racked with tumors, Obed-Edom's household was amazingly blessed.

What was the difference? In Philistia, the Philistines were trying to prove that their military victory over Israel was also a spiritual victory of Dagon over God. They had no respect for the ark or for the Lord who dwelled there, and they suffered for it. Obed-Edom, on the other hand, welcomed the ark into his house and saw nothing but blessing.

God's house is a house that must be approached with the proper respect and attitude. We cannot manipulate God or cause him to do anything for us. He is superior to us, and when we welcome him and his superiority, like Obed-Edom did, we'll see his blessing poured out upon our lives.

Prayer for the Day:

God, I want to have the heart of Obed-Edom. I respectfully welcome you into my household. Into my heart. I'm sorry for the times I've tried to manipulate or control you into doing things my way. I pray for your blessing in my heart and in my household. I love you, Lord.

AMEN.

DAY 12: Better Is One Day in Your Courts

Better is one day in your courts than a thousand elsewhere; I would rather be a doorkeeper in the house of my God than dwell in the tents of the wicked. For the LORD God is a sun and shield; the LORD bestows favor and honor; no good thing does he withhold from those whose walk is blameless.

—PSALM 84:10–11

Better is God's favor.

Ken Brown is the youngest owner-operator in the history of the McDonald's Corporation, but he didn't get there overnight. As a kid growing up in severe poverty, Ken always had a dream to own his own restaurant, and there came a critical time in his life when he had to make a decision that wound up determining his fate.

Ken was working for a large food broker, making a very good salary with a lot of company perks. But his heart was still in owning his own restaurant, and when he saw a swank Italian bistro being constructed, he decided to do something drastic: He wanted to see firsthand what it took to open a restaurant, so he laid down his great corporate job and started waiting tables at the new place.

The decision paid off for him. He was a star waiter, and people would wait in line just to have him be their server. One such person happened to be a vice president of McDonald's, and soon she invited Ken to oversee four stores. He later became an owner of two restaurants.

Just like Ken Brown, we must learn to have our priorities in line. The psalmist said he would rather have a lowly job in the house of God than to have his own bedroom with the wicked people. Ken Brown decided to have a lowly job in pursuit of his God-given calling than to waste his time on something that wasn't for him.

And the key thing to remember comes at the passage's heart and at the end of Ken Brown's story: "The Lord bestows favor and honor."

Our job is only to serve him, and let him give us favor in his timing.

Prayer for the Day:

Dear God, I thank you that no job is too small. No matter where I am, if I'm doing what you've asked me to do, then I'm in the right place, and you're seeing my efforts. I trust you to bestow favor and honor on me in due time and, in the meantime, give me the strength to serve you with all my might. I love you, Lord.

AMEN.

DAY 13: Than Thousands Elsewhere

But do not forget this one thing, dear friends: With the Lord a day is like a thousand years, and a thousand years are like a day. The Lord is not slow in keeping his promise, as some understand slowness. He is patient with you, not wanting anyone to perish, but everyone to come to repentance.

—2 Peter 3:8-9

Better is God's patience.

Jack knew a thing or two about driving downtown. All the streets were one way, alternating in direction. He'd memorized the entire layout, so he knew how to get from one point to another with the least amount of turning. And most of all, he knew the exact timing of the stoplights.

Jack knew that if he drove twenty-two miles per hour downtown, he would never have to stop at a light. Every light would turn green just before he needed to stop for it. Jack put this knowledge to use every time he drove downtown, and he always got a kick out of the impatient drivers next to him.

The scenario was inevitable. Jack would enter downtown and start at a red light. Another car would stop in the lane next to him. The light would turn green, and the other car would rev its engine to get up to speed while Jack would just cruise up to twenty-two and then stay there. The other car, in the lead, would get to the next light, which was red, and stop, with Jack bringing up the rear. The light would change, and Jack would cruise through it and past the other car. Repeat for every single light in downtown.

To the people in that other car, Jack looked slow. But we know he wasn't being slow; he was being patient.

Sometimes in our lives, we're just gunning it to get to the next red light. But when we make a conscious decision to slow down and start operating on God's timetable, we begin to see the difference between slowness and patience.

Time means nothing to God. One day or a thousand years—they're both the same. He is patient. Would that we could be the same.

Prayer for the Day:

God, you're so great. You exist outside of time, and that's kind of weird to me. Sometimes I forget that you have no restraints on time. When things are looking kind of last second to me, well, there is no such thing as "last second" to you. Help me to remember this, Lord. Help me not to mistake your patience as slowness. I want to see you as you are.

Amen.

DAY 14: Than Thousands Elsewhere

Jesus continued: "There was a man who had two sons. The younger one said to his father, 'Father, give me my share of the estate.' So he divided his property between them. Not long after that, the younger son got together all he had, set off for a distant country and there squandered his wealth in wild living. After he had spent everything, there was a severe famine in that whole country, and he began to be in need. So he went and hired himself out to a citizen of that country, who sent him to his fields to feed pigs. He longed to fill his stomach with the pods that the pigs were eating, but no one gave him anything. When he came to his senses, he said, 'How many of my father's hired men have food to spare, and here I am starving to death! I will set out and go back to my father and say to him: Father, I have sinned against heaven and against you. I am no longer worthy to be called your son; make me like one of your hired men.' So he got up and went to his father."

—LUKE 15:11–20

Better is God's forgiveness.

Sometimes we just have the entirely wrong perspective on things. We can look at the world and it starts to look pretty good. All that sinful fun out there—well, it certainly seems like it'd be better than this boring, restrictive Christian life, right?

That's the perspective the Prodigal Son had, seen in one of Jesus' most famous parables and in today's passage. The son looked into what the world had and thought it looked pretty good. So, he got his inheritance early and, in no time at all, blew all his money on riotous living.

It wasn't long before he was eating pig food and regretting his decision. He decided he'd rather *work* in his dad's house as a lowly servant than do what he was doing.

So he headed homeward and, we later learn, was welcomed with open arms. He started his journey with the wrong perspective, but a view of life from the very bottom of the barrel helped clarify the right perspective in his mind. He now knew what he'd left behind in his father's house, that life in the world wasn't as fun as it looked, and that maybe the restrictions he had at home were for his benefit.

God is good, and he forgives us, just like the Prodigal Son's father forgave him. This story, if nothing else, shows us God's miraculous forgiveness and serves as a reminder that a thousand days elsewhere is nothing compared to just one day with our loving Father.

Prayer for the Day:

God, I love you. Thank you for looking out for me. Thank you for caring for me. Thank you for receiving me as your child. Thank you so much for your forgiveness. I know I've messed up in the past, just like everyone else, and I'm so grateful for your forgiveness. Help me to walk in that forgiveness toward others today.

AMEN.

DAY 15: One Thing I Ask and I Would Seek

One thing I ask of the LORD, this is what I seek: that I may dwell in the house of the LORD all the days of my life, to gaze upon the beauty of the LORD and to seek him in his temple. For in the day of trouble he will keep me safe in his dwelling; he will hide me in the shelter of his tabernacle and set me high upon a rock. Then my head will be exalted above the enemies who surround me; at his tabernacle will I sacrifice with shouts of joy; I will sing and make music to the LORD.

—**PSALM 27:4–6**

Better is God's exaltation.

What a wish list. Let's take a look at what the psalmist is hoping for in today's passage:

to live with God forever
to see God's beauty
to worship God in his own temple
to have safety in God's house
to have refuge in God's shelter
to be exalted to high status
to shout for joy
to sing and make music just for God

That's a lot to cram into just three verses.

And yet David, whom God called a "man after his own heart" (1 Sam. 13:14; cf. Acts 13:22), puts forth this list as something worth seeking after. It's nice to dream, isn't it?

But what if this isn't just some of David's wishful thinking? What if these things were actually attainable? How would we go about doing them?

The answer lies within this very passage: It all hinges on God. Let's look again:

to live with God forever (only possible if God allows it)
to see God's beauty (again, only if God allows it)
to worship God in his own temple (if God grants permission)
to have safety in God's house (provided by God)
to have refuge in God's shelter (again, provided by God)
to be exalted to high status (set up there by God)
to shout for joy (considered a sacrificial act of worship)
to sing and make music just for God (worship again)

So the wish list isn't so far fetched, but God is the one to grant the wishes. He is the one to exalt us. It isn't too late to ask him.

Prayer for the Day:

Lord God, I thank you for your love for me. I thank you that you want to exalt me, that you long to exalt me. Help me to live in such a way that I can be on the receiving end of your exaltation. Help me to recognize it when you do exalt me in whatever way you see fit. I love you and I trust you.

Amen.

DAY 16: To See Your Beauty

The Mighty One, God, the LORD, speaks and summons the earth from the rising of the sun to the place where it sets. From Zion, perfect in beauty, God shines forth.

—PSALM 50:1–2

Better is God's judgment.

"Perfect in beauty." Sounds like a phrase one would use to describe the love of one's life. Or a newborn infant. Or perhaps a flawless bouquet of flowers, or a majestic range of lush mountains, or the starry field of the sky on a moonless country night. There are a few things on this earth that could be described as "perfect in beauty." Things without flaw or imperfection, things that are unlike anything else anywhere.

But a God of judgment?

Here's something interesting to note about this particular psalm: The first few verses describe God's beauty, and then the rest of it is about his judging Israel, using phrases like, "O Israel ... I will testify against you," and "I will rebuke you and accuse you to your face." There are some seriously harsh words that follow the description of God as "perfect in beauty."

And there's where the phrase begins to make sense. God is perfect. Absolutely perfect. Only he is capable of judging, because only he is perfect enough to declare himself a judge. God's beauty is not something to be possessed or obtained; it is perfect.

One day, we will see that beauty in all its perfection, and we will be overawed.

Prayer for the Day:

Jesus, you are perfect in beauty. I appreciate the beauty you've filled the earth with, and I realize that it all points in some small measure to your own beauty. You are perfect in beauty, Lord, and I just ask you that I might see your beauty reflected in my life. When I look at your creation, help me to see your beauty, and where I need rebuke, Lord, please remove the ugliness of my own heart.

AMEN.

DAY 17: To Find You in the Place Your Glory Dwells

I wash my hands in innocence, and go about your altar, O LORD, proclaiming aloud your praise and telling of all your wonderful deeds. I love the house where you live, O LORD, the place where your glory dwells.

—PSALM 26:6–8

Better is God's house.

This is yet another psalm of David from which the song draws its theme, and this one begins with four very powerful, pregnant words: "Vindicate me, O LORD." In this psalm, David is crying out to God for vindication from sinners and bloodthirsty men who apparently wanted to ruin him.

David, even in the midst of false accusation, doesn't start sputtering out protest or words of defense to those accusations. Instead, he appeals to God. He draws strength in the turmoil by washing his hands and heading to the altar of the Lord.

He spends some time in worship of the Lord. He spends some time in God's house.

Now, David didn't have the extreme aid we have; if he wanted to interact with God, he had to go to the tabernacle, to the place where God's glory dwelt. But through Christ's sacrifice, we can commune with God in worship anywhere we choose. Our bedrooms, our cars, our backyards can all become temporary tabernacles.

They can become God's house.

Make no mistake: We will encounter turmoil in this life. There will be times when we need to be vindicated. And in those times, we can remember David and his method of gaining strength in the hard times: a trip to God's house.

Prayer for the Day:

O Lord, I'm in awe of you. The fact that you commune with me … it's astounding, Lord. Thank you for opening up this line of communication with me. Thank you for giving me the ability and the access to worship you. I pray that your glory will dwell in me today, Lord, and that I will show that glory to everyone I encounter.

Amen.

DAY 18: One Thing I Ask and I Would Seek

The Jews still did not believe that he had been blind and had received his sight until they sent for the man's parents. "Is this your son?" they asked. "Is this the one you say was born blind? How is it that now he can see?" "We know he is our son," the parents answered, "and we know he was born blind. But how he can see now, or who opened his eyes, we don't know. Ask him. He is of age; he will speak for himself." His parents said this because they were afraid of the Jews, for already the Jews had decided that anyone who acknowledged that Jesus was the Christ would be put out of the synagogue. That was why his parents said, "He is of age; ask him." A second time they summoned the man who had been blind. "Give glory to God," they said. "We know this man is a sinner." He replied, "Whether he is a sinner or not, I don't know. One thing I do know. I was blind but now I see!"

—John 9:18–25

Better is God's power.

Here's the story: There was a man in Jerusalem who had been born blind, and Jesus healed the man by forming some mud out of clay, putting it on the man's eyes, and then having the man wash in a pool called Siloam.

Understandably, this healing caused a great stir among the people, because everyone knew the man and that he had been born blind. So the Pharisees began to investigate the healing in order to disprove that Jesus is really God's Son, but much to their dismay, they couldn't get the answer they wanted. He'd been a direct recipient of God's power, and he was just too excited to play their game.

They'd already asked the man who he thought Jesus was, and the man had already answered that he was a prophet. So then, in our passage, they try to trap the man into saying something condemning about Jesus, but the man just says, "Hey, I don't know anything about him being a sinner or not; all I know is that I was blind, but now I can see!"

Here was a guy who was a demonstration of God's power in action, and he became a great example to all of us. When we encounter disbelief among non-Christians, we don't need to try to beat them over the head with theology; we can simply tell our story. We can give them our version of "I was once blind, but now I see."

That is the one thing we do know above all else: how God has displayed his power in our lives. There is nothing more powerful than our personal stories.

Prayer for the Day:

Lord, thank you so much for exhibiting your power in my life. Thank you for turning me in the right direction. Thank you for my wonderful testimony to your greatness. Give me the strength and boldness to rely on my testimony, to deliver it in a way that people will seek you. Help me to tell my story, how I was blind, but now I see.

AMEN.

DAY 19: To See Your Beauty

Then I saw a new heaven and a new earth, for the first heaven and the first earth had passed away, and there was no longer any sea. I saw the Holy City, the new Jerusalem, coming down out of heaven from God, prepared as a bride beautifully dressed for her husband. And I heard a loud voice from the throne saying, "Now the dwelling of God is with men, and he will live with them. They will be his people, and God himself will be with them and be their God. He will wipe every tear from their eyes. There will be no more death or mourning or crying or pain, for the old order of things has passed away."

—**REVELATION 21:1–4**

Better is God's dwelling.

Nerves. Jared was a bundle of nerves. The tuxedo rental shop had gotten the color of his tie and cummerbund wrong, but he was so nervous he didn't even care. He smoothed his sweaty palms over the front of his expansion-waist pants and did his best to breathe deeply.

The card! Where was the card? He'd written his vows on it that morning, and now he couldn't find it! He searched his memory for a moment and then realized he'd left it on the kitchen table. Just what he needed—one more thing to worry about, one more thing to add to his already nerve-racked afternoon.

At least he'd wind up married at the end of it.

Finally, the time came for Jared to head to the altar. His mind began to swim with nerves, and he was barely able to follow the minister out to the place where he was supposed to stand. He lost track of his faculties and vaguely noticed the pianist begin to play and the bridesmaids begin to walk down the aisle.

And then it happened. He saw his bride. There in the back. There she was. Standing next to her father.

She'd never seemed more beautiful.

Suddenly, the nerves melted away. The anxiety, the tension—gone. Jared gazed at his wife-to-be and felt a sensation of peace he'd never known. Forever, with her, was about to start.

God's dwelling is just like that. In today's passage, we see that the city God made—heaven—is as beautiful as a bride. All Jared needed on his wedding day was to see his bride, and then everything was all right.

Can we even begin to imagine how we'll feel when we get our first glimpse of the beauty that is heaven?

Prayer for the Day:

O Lord, you're beautiful. And you've made a beautiful place for us to dwell with you. I love how this passage today says you're going to be with us and give us a tear-free existence. I can't wait, Lord. But until the day when the old order passes away, keep this vision in front of my eyes. Remind me of how it all ends, Lord. An eternity with you.

AMEN.

DAY 17: To Find You in the Place Your Glory Dwells

The Word became flesh and made his dwelling among us. We have seen his glory, the glory of the One and Only, who came from the Father, full of grace and truth.

—JOHN 1:14

Better is God's plan.

When we make plans to do something—say, go on a driving vacation—we tend to use a little logic. We map out our route; we budget for gas and food; we arrange for lodging at a hotel or with friends or relatives. In short, we do things that *make sense*.

And then there's God, who does things the crazy way. Or so it would appear.

God knew mankind needed to be redeemed, so he sent his Son? Took the biggest risk of all time and became flesh, just like us? Laid the entire human race, and his own reputation, on the line just because he loved us?

Yes.

In fact, God had it in the works the whole time.

It was always in God's design to make his dwelling among us. He did it with the Israelites in the Old Testament, dwelling with them in the tabernacle and then in the temple. When Jesus came to earth, it was just an extension of God's original design. Except this time he was in the form of a man.

God's plan was to come to earth so that we might see his glory firsthand. He had to do it in order to open a way for us to come to him. He had a plan, and it was a glorious one.

If we can find no other reason than this, it is still a most compelling reason to worship him.

Prayer for the Day:

God. Jesus. Thank you for making your dwelling among us. Thank you for emptying yourself out and for becoming flesh. Thank you for giving it all on that cross. I don't understand your plans sometimes, but I'm thankful that you are in control and not me. I trust your plan, Lord. I love you.

AMEN.

DAY 21: My Heart and Flesh Cry Out

How lovely is your dwelling place, O LORD Almighty! My soul yearns, even faints, for the courts of the LORD; my heart and my flesh cry out for the living God.

—PSALM 84:1-2

Better is God's court.

Today's passage is full of some intense words, talking about yearning and fainting and crying out for God. It's easy to gloss over these words when they appear so matter-of-factly, so take a moment to go back and reread the passage as if it were really you expressing these sentiments and not the psalmist who wrote them.

Do our souls yearn for the courts of the Lord? Do we crave them with all that is in us, until we faint? Do we ache for contact with the Holy One? Do we cry out for him from the depths of all that is within us?

This is how we should feel.

The courts of the Lord are such a blessed place. And the reason our hearts and our flesh cry out for the living God is because his presence is exactly what they were made to desire. We were made to commune with God, to seek him with everything we have until we find him.

We long for a relationship with him because that is exactly what he created us to do.

And one blessed day, we will all find what we've been looking for. Our heart's cry will be answered. Our soul's yearnings will be satisfied. We will be welcomed into heaven with open arms.

It is truly so much better there.

Prayer for the Day:

Lord God, thank you for making a place for me. Thank you for welcoming me into a relationship with you, for giving my soul something to look forward to. I love you so much, and I can't wait to get to heaven, the place where my heart longs to be. Thank you for giving me the hope of eternity; help me to treasure it while I'm here.

Amen.

DAY 22: My Heart and Flesh Cry Out

Woe to them, because they have strayed from me! Destruction to them, because they have rebelled against me! I long to redeem them but they speak lies against me. They do not cry out to me from their hearts but wail upon their beds. They gather together for grain and new wine but turn away from me.

—HOSEA 7:13–14

Better is God's redemption.

Hosea's story is an interesting one. Here is a prophet, living in a time of acute Israelite apostasy, whom God tells to marry a prostitute.

Yes. Marry a prostitute.

Hosea obeys and marries Gomer, a prostitute. Marriage does nothing to change her ways, and eventually she is led astray and into apparent slavery. And then Hosea, in an amazing act of love, purchases her back from her enslavement and treats her more lovingly than she could ever deserve.

She had turned her back on Hosea, and though it tore him up, he still pursued her and redeemed her in an effort to show her his total love.

This is how God loves us.

Though we turn away from him at times for other pursuits, he still loves us. He longs to redeem us even when, in our sin, we speak lies against him. When we ignore him and abstain from crying out to him, he *still* longs to love us.

His redemptive love makes as much sense as the love of a husband for his prostitute wife. It defies logic, yet at the heart level, it's understandable. It's the unbreakable bond of a covenant.

God's redemptive love is so strong that not even our sinful adultery can quell it.

Prayer for the Day:

God, my heart and flesh do cry out to you. I'm amazed at how persistent your redemption is, and I do acknowledge that I, at times, act like a prostitute wife. Thank you for loving me in spite of my sin, and thank you for redeeming me. Help me to live a life that is pleasing to you; help me to honor you in all I do. I love you.

AMEN.

DAY 23: For You the Living God

The angel said to the women, "Do not be afraid, for I know that you are looking for Jesus, who was crucified. He is not here; he has risen, just as he said. Come and see the place where he lay. Then go quickly and tell his disciples: 'He has risen from the dead and is going ahead of you into Galilee. There you will see him.' Now I have told you."

—**MATTHEW 28:5-7**

Better is God's victory.

What an amazing feat! God is not dead; he is alive.

In our Christian culture, this phrase has become so commonplace that it's almost lost its meaning. "Jesus is alive" sometimes sounds as compelling to our ears as "Good morning."

But it's true. Jesus *is* alive! He is not a corpse in a tomb somewhere. He is not an idol carved by human hands. He is not a lifeless spirit on some other plane of existence.

He is real.

He is alive.

Can you imagine what it must have been like for those women who came to visit Jesus' tomb, only to find an angel there, telling them what was really going on? His words point us toward a potent truth: Death couldn't hold Jesus down.

Other men have been worshipped beyond their deaths. Jesus is the only one who *didn't stay dead*. Make no mistake: There have been some great men in history, men whose stories can inspire us to great heights. But there has been only one man who died, came back to life, and then ascended into heaven.

Jesus is alive. He fought a tooth-and-nail battle with death itself and came out victorious. He hammered death and achieved a life-giving victory.

**Jesus is the living God.
Let us worship him!**

Prayer for the Day:

Jesus, you're so tough. I believe in you. I believe you died on the cross and you slugged it out with death and came out on top. I believe you are alive, and I love that about you. Thank you for giving me life through your death. Thank you for loving me.

                                 AMEN.

DAY 24: Your Spirit's Water for My Soul

As the deer pants for streams of water, so my soul pants for you, O God. My soul thirsts for God, for the living God. When can I go and meet with God?

—PSALM 42:1–2

Better is God's stream.

Deer are majestic animals, full of grace. And they are quite amazing in another respect: Unlike cows, sheep, and other cud-chewing animals, deer have antlers instead of horns. Their antlers grow every year after mating season, and because of the nutrition required to grow those antlers, deer are very selective eaters, generally feeding on leaves, twigs, and fruit.

And all that food can make a deer mighty thirsty.

Deer are also enormous drinkers; water, being necessary for life, is also first and foremost on their minds for that antler growth. The water sustains them, helps them digest their food and get the most out of it, and, just as for the rest of us, keeps them healthy.

They must have it.

God's Spirit is similar to water. His Spirit refreshes us and rejuvenates us and helps us to do a little growing ourselves. Deer need water, so do we.

Interestingly, in today's psalm, the psalmist was offering a prayer for deliverance from his oppressors. Deer, being widely hunted, still have to stop and take in some water in order to stay on the run from their pursuers. Even in the midst of the hunt, they must stop and focus on their sustaining water.

God's stream of refreshing is the perfect place to rest, even in the midst of oppression from our enemy. His Spirit truly is water to our souls.

Prayer for the Day:

Restore my soul, O God. Refresh me. Rejuvenate me. I love you, Lord, and I'm so thirsty for you. I cry out to you to quench my spiritual thirst. Just like the deer longs for water, Lord, I long for you. Help me to grow. Help me to thrive. Help me this day.

Amen.

DAY 25: Your Spirit's Water for My Soul

When a Samaritan woman came to draw water, Jesus said to her, "Will you give me a drink?" (His disciples had gone into the town to buy food.) The Samaritan woman said to him, "You are a Jew and I am a Samaritan woman. How can you ask me for a drink?" (For Jews do not associate with Samaritans.) Jesus answered her, "If you knew the gift of God and who it is that asks you for a drink, you would have asked him and he would have given you living water." "Sir," the woman said, "you have nothing to draw with and the well is deep. Where can you get this living water? Are you greater than our father Jacob, who gave us the well and drank from it himself, as did also his sons and his flocks and herds?" Jesus answered, "Everyone who drinks this water will be thirsty again, but whoever drinks the water I give him will never thirst. Indeed, the water I give him will become in him a spring of water welling up to eternal life."

—JOHN 4:7–14

Better is God's eternal life.

Whenever Michelle is feeling a little run down, a little sapped of energy and strength, she has a trick to get back on top. This little trick also works for her whenever she feels a slight cold coming on, or some other virus or bacteria that threatens her day-to-day health.

She juices.

To Michelle, there's something about drinking some fresh juice that awakens her body and causes it to triumph over whatever is bringing her down. Whether it's something complicated like carrot-apple-ginger-lemon juice or just a few oranges down the hatch, Michelle derives life from drinking something that is already alive.

This is but a pale imitation of the life Jesus offers.

Juiced fruit and vegetables are fine in their own right, but those will eventually decay and, if left long enough, become downright detrimental.

But Jesus offers us life from a well of living water, and when we drink it, we receive eternal life.

Jesus offers us entrance into heaven. It is so much better than anything we could ever conceive on our own.

Better is God's life.

Prayer for the Day:

Jesus, thank you for that eternal life you offer, even to the outsiders like the Samaritans. And me. I pray that your life will dwell within me and give me life. Except, go beyond that, Lord. Take me further, God. I submit to you and your plan, and I will do whatever it takes to follow you into eternal life.

AMEN.

DAY 26: I've Tasted and I've Seen

Taste and see that the LORD is good; blessed is the man who takes refuge in him.

—PSALM 34:8

Better is God's goodness.

In his famous book *The Lion, the Witch and the Wardrobe*, C. S. Lewis portrays Christ as a lion named Aslan, who rules the land of Narnia. And when the main characters of the book, four English children, first hear of Aslan, they wonder aloud how they could possibly interact with a lion ruler.

One of the children asks about Aslan, inquiring whether a lion could be safe to be around. The giver of information immediately responds that, no, Aslan isn't *safe*, but he is *good*.

There is a difference.

God is not safe. He is not cute and cuddly, and he is not under our command like a circus animal. He is wild, he is dangerous, he is unpredictable, to a degree.

But he is good.

We do not trust God because we can tame him; we trust him because he is good. Because we've seen that goodness at work in our own lives, in the story of Christ and the crucifixion.

We cannot for a moment think that God is at our beck and call, waiting to perform a few tricks in exchange for a treat; no, he is wild as a lion, and in following him, we follow wildness itself.

> **But he is good. Oh, so good.
> And his goodness outweighs the rest of
> the world time after time.**

Prayer for the Day:

Lord, I have tasted your goodness. I've seen it with my own eyes. I know you are good, though you are good on your terms and not on mine. Sometimes I have trouble seeing the good in you, but that's where it comes down to trust. I trust your goodness, Lord, and I believe you have my best interests at heart—every time. Help those places of my heart that are resistant to trusting you. Bring them around.

AMEN.

DAY 27: I've Tasted and I've Seen

You are the salt of the earth. But if the salt loses its saltiness, how can it be made salty again? It is no longer good for anything, except to be thrown out and trampled by men.

—**MATTHEW 5:13**

Better is God's flavor.

Saturday is a great day to go grocery shopping. Saturday is the day when supermarkets generally hand out free samples of a few items.

How many times have you purchased something after trying the sample? How many times, after tasting the sample, are you glad that you didn't spend your money on that horrible product?

Sampling works in the supermarket, and it also works in the kingdom of God. Anyone who's had a legitimate sample of what God has to offer will always come back wanting more.

But what about us? Could we be considered "samples" of the Lord? We are the closest thing to human representation he has, and we are the lens through which many unsaved people look at God.

So what will people taste when they sample us? Will they taste the saltiness of God? Will they be able to savor what makes God so special, or will they only find the blandness of the world? Will they want more, or will they be glad they haven't wasted their time?

The good thing for us is that just a little bit of salt can flavor a whole lot of blandness. We aren't called to be superheroes for Christ; we can only do our best to live a God-infused life, and his saltiness will cut through the blandness of humanity that we all carry with us.

Prayer for the Day:

Lord God, thank you for letting me be your representative to the world. For letting me be a small sample of you. I pray that you will flavor me, Lord. I know how great you are; I pray that you will help me to live out that greatness in front of the people who need to taste and see it. My friends. My family. Everyone who doesn't know you. I love you, God.

AMEN.

DAY 28: Come Once Again to Me

Do not let your hearts be troubled. Trust in God; trust also in me. In my Father's house are many rooms; if it were not so, I would have told you. I am going there to prepare a place for you. And if I go and prepare a place for you, I will come back and take you to be with me that you also may be where I am. You know the way to the place where I am going.

—John 14:1–4

Better is God's preparation.

What hope this passage brings! We are not to let our hearts be troubled, because we have a hope that the unsaved do not. We have the hope of an eternity with Jesus.

And we have the hope that comes from knowing that he's coming back. We don't know when, but he is coming back.

Look at how Jesus puts it: "If I go and prepare a place for you, I will come back and take you to be with me." He wouldn't go through the trouble of all that preparation if he had no intention of coming back for us. He will do what he says; because we know that, we know he will come once again to us.

He's coming back!

It is in our times of trouble, our times of depression, our times when we are at our lowest, full of despondency and despair, that we can remember this verse and draw strength and hope from it. It is when our hearts become troubled that we can reflect upon the very words and promises of Jesus—and know that he will return for us.

It is only a matter of time.

**Let us worship him for his preparation!
Let us praise him for his promises!**

Prayer for the Day:

Lord, I think about this verse, and my heart starts fluttering. I can't even fathom what that will be like, to spend eternity with you in a place you made just for me. It's just so crazy, Lord. Jesus, thank you for giving me this hope; thank you for giving me something to hold on to when my world starts spinning like crazy. Thank you. Thank you. Thank you for promising to come back. I can't wait.

AMEN.

DAY 29: I Will Draw Near to You

The law is only a shadow of the good things that are coming—not the realities themselves. For this reason it can never, by the same sacrifices repeated endlessly year after year, make perfect those who draw near to worship. If it could, would they not have stopped being offered? For the worshipers would have been cleansed once for all, and would no longer have felt guilty for their sins. But those sacrifices are an annual reminder of sins, because it is impossible for the blood of bulls and goats to take away sins.

—Hebrews 10:1–4

Better is God's sacrifice.

In the Old Testament, no one could draw near to God without a sacrifice. God set up the Mosaic law, the writer of Hebrews tells us, as a shadow of the good things that are coming—the law of Christ. The easier yoke.

Christ made the final sacrifice for us.

It is impossible to draw near to God without accepting the sacrifice of Christ. The Old Testament sacrifices were never enough to cleanse anyone fully. They were never enough to make things completely right with God. And then along came Jesus, and he became the very sacrifice that Old Testament worshippers had to offer annually.

Except this time, it took only one sacrifice. Jesus doesn't have to die once a year; he doesn't have to die ever again.

Once and for all.

It's only through the blood of Christ that we can draw near to God. We have reminders of our sins, but thankfully, we also have these words as reminders of what Christ did for us. Of the sacrifice he made, so that we might be able to draw near to him.

What a precious price. What a marvelous gift.

He paid dearly for us to have the opportunity; let us draw near to him.

Prayer for the Day:

Lord Jesus Christ, thank you so much for making the sacrifice once for all of us. I'm so glad I'm included in that sacrifice. You're so inclusive, Lord, and I'm very grateful for it. Lord, I take this time right now to be quiet and to draw near to you. I pray that as I do so, you will incline your ear toward me. I love you, Lord, and I cherish this precious gift you've given me.

Amen.

DAY 29: I Will Draw Near to You

Therefore, brothers, since we have confidence to enter the Most Holy Place by the blood of Jesus, by a new and living way opened for us through the curtain, that is, his body, and since we have a great priest over the house of God, let us draw near to God with a sincere heart in full assurance of faith, having our hearts sprinkled to cleanse us from a guilty conscience and having our bodies washed with pure water. Let us hold unswervingly to the hope we profess, for he who promised is faithful. And let us consider how we may spur one another on toward love and good deeds.

—**Hebrews 10:19–24**

Better is God's faithfulness.

God is so faithful.

As we've journeyed through this wonderful song over the past month, we've learned a lot of things about God. But one thing that shines through is his great faithfulness toward us. We can trust him because he is faithful. We can love him because he is faithful. We can serve him because he is faithful. We know that when we go with God, we're going with the sure hand, the steady love.

So let us venture out into this world unafraid of what lies ahead. Let us indeed draw near to God, so that we might deliver his heart to those who need it most. Let us look toward each other in love, so that we might spur each other on to make a loving, practical difference in the lives of everyone we meet.

Let us celebrate God's faithfulness by drawing near to him. Let us grasp our faith with both hands, gripping firmly to what we know. Let us cling to the Lord for dear life, for with him we can navigate this world unswervingly.

Let us draw near to him, and in return, may he draw near to us. May we experience God in an intimate way.

For he is so much better.

Prayer for the Day:

Lord, you are better. I hold tight to your teachings, and where I don't understand something in your Word, I pray you will help me to see your heart behind it. I pray you will bless me as I interact with others today, that you will help me hold on to the faith unswervingly and to encourage my fellow Christians to live for you, as they encourage me. I pray your blessing over my life and theirs.

AMEN.

Additional copies of this and other
Honor products are available wherever good books are sold.

Other titles in the *30 Days of Worship* series:
Here I Am to Worship
Blessed Be Your Name
In Christ Alone
The Heart of Worship
Let Everything That Has Breath

If you have enjoyed this book,
or if it has had an impact on your life,
we would like to hear from you.

Please contact us at:

Honor Books
Cook Communications Ministries, Dept. 201
4050 Lee Vance View
Colorado Springs, CO 80918

Or visit our Web site:
www.cookministries.com